George Frideric Handel

SIX FUGUES OR VOLUNTARYS

for organ or harpsichord

Edited by
H. Diack Johnstone

Music Department
OXFORD UNIVERSITY PRESS
Oxford and New York

Oxford University Press, Walton Street, Oxford OX2 6DP
Oxford New York Toronto
Delhi Bombay Calcutta Madras Karachi
Petaling Jaya Singapore Hong Kong Tokyo
Nairobi Dar es Salaam Cape Town
Melbourne Auckland
and associated companies in
Beirut Berlin Ibadan Nicosia

Oxford is a trade mark of Oxford University Press

PREFACE

Sources and Textual History

Handel's *Six Fugues or Voluntarys* are nothing like so well known as they ought to be. Strongly characterized in subject matter and splendidly vital in their working out, they are among the finest keyboard fugues of the period, Bach's '48' notwithstanding. Yet, in any comparison of the two, the Handel examples have generally been found wanting. It is perfectly true that they do not adhere to the rules of strict part-writing—they cannot readily be written out in open score for instance; neither do they make any great play, stretto apart, with such standard fugal devices as augmentation, inversion and the like. But such things are by no means essential to the creation of a first-class fugue, and for Handel, always the least academic of composers, linear logic as such was relatively unimportant, as indeed it was for most other composers working within the Italian contrapuntal tradition.

Most of Handel's solo keyboard music was written within the first twenty years of the century.[1] Although not published until August 1735, so too were the *Six Fugues or Voluntarys.* The timing is doubtless coincidental, but only a couple of months earlier, Johann Mattheson, a good friend and former associate, brought out a collection of twelve fugues (and other pieces)—*Die wol-klingende Finger-Sprache*—which he dedicated to the 'deeply learned and world-famous gentleman, Georg Friedrich Händel'.[2] The Handel set makes no mention of Mattheson and cannot properly be regarded as a reciprocal gesture. It is fairly certain, however, that John Walsh had by this date become Handel's regular publisher, and thus the 1735 edition, for all its faults, must be assumed to have had the composer's authority (though he himself can hardly have seen a proof). As such it serves as copy-text for the present edition. The title-page reads as follows:

> Six FUGUES / OR / VOLUNTARYS / *for the* / ORGAN / OR / HARPSICORD / *Compos'd by* / G. F. HANDEL. / TROISIEME OVARAGE. / *London. Printed for and Sold by* I. Walsh, *Musick Printer, and Instrument maker to his Majesty, / at the Harp and Hoboy in Catherine Street in the Strand.* N°. 543

At first sight, the phrase 'Troisieme Ovarage' (*sic*) is puzzling, since Handel's real Opus 3, the six so-called 'Oboe Concertos', had already been published only nine months previously (in December 1734). The explanation, it would appear, is that this was the third such collection of Handel's keyboard music so far printed , the other two being the first and second books of *Suites de Pieces* which came out in 1720 and 1733. Although according to the *British Union-Catalogue of Early Music* (1957), a second issue of the work is to be distinguished by the correction of 'Ovarage' to 'Ouvrage' on the title-page, in fact all copies of the original Walsh edition are identical.

Apart from the Walsh, only one other edition of these pieces was printed during Handel's lifetime, and this was published by Boivin and Le Clerc in Paris under the title: SIX / FUGUES / *Pour le Clavecin / óu / L'Orgue / Par / G. F. HANDEL. / Troisieme Ouvrage* (hence, no doubt, the confusion in *BUCEM*). The generally accepted date is 1738, but since the *'Privilege General'* authorizing publication is dated 19 December of that year, it may well have been 1739 before it actually appeared. What authority, if any, it has is by no means certain; however, like one or two other Parisian Handel publications of the same period, it derives directly from Walsh.[3] Its chief interest from an editorial point of view is that it provides a few more ties and rests, corrects a couple of the more blatant errors in Fuga V, and supplies a chordal amplification of the last two bars of no. IV which, in Walsh, are given simply as a figured bass.

Of the four early eighteenth-century manuscript sources, much the most important is the autograph (British Library, RM 20 g. 14). Here the C minor fugue (no. VI) appears between nos. I and II: the latter is a fair copy, but all the rest are composition drafts showing various crossings-out and other changes of mind, and dating almost certainly from the years 1716–17. Closely related is RM 18 b. 8 (F2 in Terence Best's useful checklist of sources referred to in note 1); this is the work of an as yet unidentified scribe, and was copied, quite possibly from the autograph, only a year or two later. Here the fugues (interspersed with others from the harpsichord suites) are ordered VI, I, III, II, V and IV. This same order is also to be found in RM 19 a. 3 (Best F3), the date of which is later (1730–32), and the copyist, Larsen's S2.[4] Between them (and following the same numerical sequence) comes a manuscript owned by the Earl of Malmesbury (Best J); this was copied *c.*1727 by Larsen's Hb. 1 (and not, as has been hitherto supposed, by J. C. Smith, junior).[5] Also quite early (*c.*1732) and of some interest in that one or two readings suggest he may

[1] See Terence Best, 'Handel's harpsichord music: a checklist', in *Music in Eighteenth-Century England: Essays in Memory of Charles Cudworth* ed. Christopher Hogwood and Richard Luckett (Cambridge, 1983), pp. 171–87; also 'Die Chronologie von Händels Klaviermusik', in *Händel-Jahrbuch* xxvii (1981), pp. 79–87 and 'Handel's Keyboard Music', in *The Musical Times* cxii (September, 1971), pp. 845–8. For more on the solo organ works as such, see H. Diack Johnstone, 'Handel's Organ Voluntaries', in *The Musical Times* cxxvii (January, 1986), pp. 47–51.

[2] O. E. Deutsch, *Handel: A Documentary Biography* (London, 1955), p. 391.

[3] See Cecil Hopkinson, 'Handel and France: editions published there during his lifetime', in *Edinburgh Bibliographical Society Transactions*, Vol. III, Pt. 4 (Edinburgh, 1957), pp. 223–48.

[4] See J. P. Larsen, *Handel's Messiah: Origins, Composition, Sources* (London, 1957), p. 267.

[5] I am greatly indebted to Terence Best (editor of the Hallische Händel-Ausgabe edition of these same six fugues) for providing the most up-to-date information available on the copyists and dating of the manuscript sources, information which, in so far as the copyist of the Malmesbury MS is concerned, supersedes that given in Mr Best's own checklist (p. 177).

VORWORT

Quellen und Textüberlieferung

Händels *Six Fugues or Voluntarys* sind bei weitem nicht so bekannt wie sie es verdient hätten. Kräftig charakterisiert in ihrem thematischen Material und großartig lebendig in ihrer Ausarbeitung, gehören sie zu den hervorragendsten Fugen für Tasteninstrumente der Zeit, ungeachtet der '48' von Bach. Dennochs wurden bei jedem Vergleich beider Händels Beispiele gewöhnlich als schwächer bewertet. Es ist absolut zutreffend, daß sie sich nicht an die Regeln strenger Mehrstimmigkeit halten—beispielsweise können sie nicht ohne weiteres in Partitur ausgeschrieben werden; auch machen sie, abgesehen von der Engführung, nicht viel Gebrauch von den üblichen Kunstgriffen der Fuge wie Augmentation, Inversion und ähnlichem. Doch sind solche Dinge keinesfalls wesentlich für die Komposition einer erstklassigen Fuge, und für Händel, der unter den Komponisten stets am wenigsten akademisch genannt werden kann, war lineare Folgerichtigkeit als solche relativ unwichtig wie tatsächlich für die meisten anderen Komponisten der italienischen Kontrapunkttradition.

Das meiste von Händels solistischer Tastenmusik ist in den ersten zwanzig Jahren des Jahrhunderts entstanden.[1] Dazu gehören auch die *Six Fugues or Voluntarys,* obwohl sie nicht vor August 1735 veröffentlicht wurden. Nur wenige Monate vorher, doch zweifellos zufällig in der zeitlichen Abstimmung, brachte Johann Mattheson, ein guter Freund und früherer Kollege, eine Sammlung von zwölf Fugen (und anderen Stücken) heraus—*Die wol-klingende Finger-Sprache*—die er dem Hochgelahrten und Weltberühmten Herrn, Herrn Georg Friedrich Händel widmete.[2] Die Händel-Ausgabe erwähnt Mattheson nicht und kann strenggenommen nicht als entsprechende Geste gesehen werden. Mit ziemlicher Sicherheit aber war John Walsh zu dieser Zeit Händels regulärer Verleger geworden, und so muß angenommen werden, daß die Ausgabe von 1735 trotz all ihrer Fehler die Autorisierung des Komponisten hatte (obwohl er selbst kaum Korrekturabzüge gesehen haben kann). Als solche dient sie der vorliegenden Edition als beglaubigter Text. Das Titelblatt lautet folgendermaßen:

> Six FUGUES / OR / VOLUNTARYS / *for the* / ORGAN / OR / HARPSICORD / *Compos'd by* / G. F. HANDEL. / TROISIEME OVARAGE. / *London. Printed for and Sold by* I. Walsh, *Musick Printer, and Instrument maker to his Majesty, / at the Harp and Hoboy in Catherine Street in the Strand.* N°. 543

Auf den ersten Blick ist die Angabe 'Troisieme Ovarage' (sic) verwirrend, da Händels wirkliches Opus 3, die sechs sogenannten 'Oboen-Konzerte', gerade neun Monate vorher (Dezember 1734) herausgekommen war. Möglicherweise ist die Erklärung dafür, daß dies die dritte bis dahin gedruckte Sammlung von Händels Tastenmusik war; die beiden ersten sind das erste und zweite Buch der *Suites de Pieces,* die 1720 und 1733 erschienen. Obwohl nach dem *British Union-Catalogue of Early Music* (1957) eine zweite Ausgabe des Werkes an der Verbesserung des Wortes 'Ovarage' in 'Ouvrage' auf dem Titelblatt deutlich erkennbar ist, sind faktisch alle Exemplare der originalen Walsh–Ausgabe identisch.

Abgesehen von Walsh erschien zu Händels Lebzeiten nur eine andere Edition dieser Stücke, und zwar bei Boivin und Le Clerc in Paris unter dem Titel *SIX / FUGUES / Pour le Clavecin / óu / L'Orgue / Par / G. F. HANDEL. / Troisieme Ouvrage* (daher zweifellos die Verwechslung in *BUCEM*). Das allgemein angenommene Datum ist 1738, doch da der die Veröffentlichung genehmigende *'Privilege General'* am 19. Dezember dieses Jahres datiert ist, könnte das tatsächliche Erscheinungsjahr auch 1739 sein. Welche Art Autorisierung, wenn überhaupt, diese Edition hat, ist keineswegs sicher; doch steht sie, wie zwei andere Pariser Händel–Ausgaben, in direktem Zusammenhang mit Walsh.[3] Vom herausgeberischen Standpunkt ist sie hauptsächlich interessant, weil sie einige weitere Haltebögen und Pausen liefert, einige der schlimmsten Fehler in Fuge V korrigiert und eine akkordische Ausfüllung der letzten zwei Takte von Nr. IV ergänzt, die bei Walsh lediglich als bezifferter Baß wiedergegeben sind.

Von den vier handschriftlichen Quellen des frühen 18. Jahrhunderts ist das Autograph die bei weitem bedeutendste (British Library, RM 20 g. 14). Darin steht die c-moll-Fuge (Nr. VI) zwischen Nr. I und Nr. II: letztere ist eine Reinschrift, alle anderen sind Kompositionsskizzen mit verschiedenen Durchstreichungen und inhaltlichen Änderungen, die mit ziemlicher Sicherheit aus den Jahren 1716/17 stammen. In enger Beziehung dazu steht RM 18 b. 8 (F2 in dem nützlichen Quellenverzeichnis von Terence Best, s. Fußnote 1); sie ist die Arbeit eines bisher nicht identifizierten Schreibers und wurde nur ein oder zwei Jahre später abgeschrieben, sehr wahrscheinlich vom Autograph. Die Anordnung der Fugen (mit anderen aus den Cembalo-Suiten durchsetzt) ist: VI, I, III, II, V und IV. Diese Anordnung bringt auch RM 19 a. 3 (Best F3), die später (1730–1732) zu datieren ist und von Larsens S2 geschrieben wurde.[4] Zwis-

[1] Vgl. Terence Best, 'Handel's harpsichord music: a checklist', in: *Music in Eighteenth-Century England: Essays in Memory of Charles Cudworth,* hrsg. von Christopher Hogwood und Richard Luckett (Cambridge, 1983), S. 171–187; ebenso 'Die Chronologie von Händels Klaviermusik', in: *Händel-Jahrbuch* 27 (1981), S. 79–87, und 'Handel's Keyboard Music', in: *The Musical Times* 112 (September 1971), S. 845–848. Für weitere Informationen zu den Werken für Orgel solo s. H. Diack Johnstone, 'Handel's Organ Voluntaries', in: *The Musical Times* 127 (Januar 1986), S. 47–51.

[2] O. E. Deutsch, *Handel: A Documentary Biography* (London, 1955), S. 391.

[3] Vgl. Cecil Hopkinson, 'Handel and France: editions published there during his lifetime', in: *Edinburgh Bibliographical Society Transactions,* Bd. 3, Teil 4 (Edinburgh, 1957), S. 223–248.

[4] Vgl. J. P. Larsen, *Handel's Messiah: Origins, Composition, Sources* (London, 1957), S. 267.

possibly have had sight of the autograph is a copy of nos. II and III by John Reading (c.1685–1764), sometime organist of Dulwich College; these are still preserved in the library there (MS 92 d.), but have no textual authority.

No fewer than four of the six pieces in this collection appear in an alternative form elsewhere. Even before publication in its keyboard version, the G major fugue (no. II) had already been arranged for orchestra (though so clumsily it can hardly have been the work of Handel himself) as the last movement of the concerto Op. 3 no. 3.[6] Likewise no. III is a somewhat expanded version of a movement which had previously served as part of the opening Sinfonia to the Brockes Passion (1716) and was, in that form, to turn up again as the third movement of Op. 3 no. 2. No. VI on the other hand was later reduced to three parts, transposed up a fifth to G minor, and re-written (in doubled time-values) to become the second movement of the trio sonata Op. 5 no. 5 (1738), while the foreshortened re-working of no. V is even more drastic—as the chorus, 'They loathed to drink of the river', in the oratorio *Israel in Egypt* (1738 also).

Despite the numerous errors in the 1735 Walsh edition—and some are wildly wrong—the plates were never corrected. After Walsh's death (in 1766), they passed to Hermond Wright who reprinted them, unaltered but for the imprint, in about 1785. They were still in use some 25 years later, as witness the edition 'Printed & Sold by [Thomas] Preston, at his Wholesale Warehouses, 97, Strand' (c.1810). In the meantime, two further English editions had appeared, one issued by James Harrison as part of his *New Musical Magazine* [1784], the other by Samuel Arnold in the 131st fascicle of his complete Handel edition (c.1793); both are quite obviously based on Walsh, each with its own further crop of misprints.

Three other late eighteenth-century editions ought also to be mentioned, though curiously only the first is included by William C. Smith in his comprehensive *Handel: A Descriptive Catalogue of the Early Editions* (1960; rev. 2/1970). This is a collection of *Quatorze Fugues Pour Clavecin ou Piano* printed by Imbault in Paris round about 1790, and in addition to the six fugues under discussion, it includes another five from the *Suites de Pieces* plus three more arranged for keyboard from Op. 6 nos. 1, 6 and 11. The other two are both German. Neither has any authority, yet both are of considerable interest in being textually independent not only of the earlier Walsh (and Boivin/Le Clerc) editions, but also of each other, and to some extent the manuscript sources as well. The first (*VI Fugen / von / HENDEL / für / Componisten Organisten / und / Liebhaber der höhern Musik*) was published at Darmstadt in 1787, presumably by the firm of Krämer & Bossler, the second (*SIX FUGUES / pour le / CLAVECIN ou L'ORGUE / composées par / G. F. Händel*) by Leopold Kozeluch in Vienna only two years later.[7] Of the several nineteenth-century editions, only the Chrysander text of 1859 (in volume 2 of the Händel-Gesellschaft edition) has any real claim to scholarship, and that, it now appears, was based not on any of the original sources considered here, but rather on the [1848] Peters edition ('nouvelle revue et corrigée critiquement') with which it is virtually identical.

Editorial Method

With the exception of the Malmesbury MS, the variant readings of which have been kindly communicated by Terence Best, every one of the sources listed above has been carefully examined by the present editor. None, not even the autograph, is entirely accurate in every respect. Primacy therefore rests with the 1735 Walsh edition which, as we have already remarked, evidently had the composer's *imprimatur*, and it is this text, purged of errors, which is reproduced here. To it, however, are added a fair number of rests, ties, accidentals and even occasional notes drawn from those other sources which, being either earlier than or more or less contemporary with the print, may be considered to have some measure of authority—most obviously of course the autograph, but also (in descending order of importance), F2, F3, J and the 1738 Paris edition. All such additions are clearly distinguished by the use of parentheses (i.e. round brackets). Anything printed small or enclosed within square brackets on the other hand is wholly editorial; so too are all crossed ties, lines indicating voice-leading, and half brackets used to clarify the distribution of parts between the hands. Accidentals in the copytext which are redundant in terms of the modern convention (whereby accidentals not specifically cancelled remain in force throughout the bar) have been silently omitted, as have a very few redundant rests and superfluous double stemming also. By the same token, those accidentals not actually present in any of the early sources are shown as editorial. All other deviations from the Walsh edition together with some of the more important variants in the secondary sources are tabled in the final section headed 'Critical Commentary'.

Interpretation and Performance

In all the sources, both printed and manuscript, the only ornament sign used is *tr* (or ⁓), and that only in Fuga I. There is, however, no reason why a few extra trills (and even the occasional mordent) should not be added, and there are a number of suggestions to this effect enclosed in editorial square brackets. These some players will choose to ignore, while others may wish to carry the process still further. Except where closing notes are already built into the notation (as in no. I, bb. 13 and 65), most

[6] See Donald Burrows, 'Walsh's editions of Handel's Opera 1–5: the texts and their sources', in *Music in Eighteenth-Century England* ed. Hogwood and Luckett (Cambridge, 1983), pp. 87–90.

[7] Copies the latter are to be found in the British Library (press-mark e. 438 b. (1)) and in the collection of Gerald Coke, Esq., Bentley, Hants. The identification of Kozeluch as publisher I owe to Dr Alan Tyson of All Souls College, Oxford. There is no copy of the 1787 Darmstadt edition in this country; I am grateful therefore to Mr Victor Cardell who kindly supplied a xerox of the one at Yale (University Music Library).

chen diesen beiden Handschriften (mit derselben Nummernfolge) steht ein Manuskript im Besitz des Earl of Malmesbury (Best J), das um 1727 von Larsens Hb. 1 geschrieben wurde (und nicht, wie bisher angenommen, von J. C. Smith junior).[5] Ziemlich früh (um 1732) und recht interessant ist auch eine Abschrift von Nr. II und Nr. III durch John Reading (um 1685–1764), der einige Zeit Organist in Dulwich College war. Das Manuskript wird in der dortigen Bibliothek aufbewahrt (MS 92 d.); es enthält keinen autorisierten Text, doch lassen ein oder zwei Lesarten darauf schließen, daß der Schreiber vielleicht das Autograph hat einsehen können.

Nicht weniger als vier der sechs Stücke dieser Sammlung kommen auch in anderer Form vor. Die G-Dur-Fuge (Nr. II) wurde sogar vor ihrer Veröffentlichung in der Version für Tasteninstrument für Orchester bearbeitet (allerdings so ungeschickt, daß sie kaum die Arbeit von Händel selbst sein kann) als letzter Satz des Konzerts op. 3 Nr. 3.[6] Ebenso ist Nr. III eine etwas erweiterte Version eines Satzes, der vorher als Teil der Eröffnungs-Sinfonia zur Brockes-Passion (1716) diente und der in dieser Form als dritter Satz von op. 3 Nr. 2 wieder auftaucht. Nr. VI wiederum wurde später auf frei Stimmen reduziert, eine Quinte hinauf nach g-moll transponiert und neu geschrieben (in doppelten Zeitwerten) als zweiter Satz der Triosonate op. 5 Nr. 5 (1738), während die verkürzende Umarbeitung von Nr. V noch drastischer verfährt—als Chor 'They loathed to drink of the river' im Oratorium *Israel in Egypt* (ebenfalls 1738).

Ungeachtet der zahlreichen Fehler in der Ausgabe von Walsh 1735—und einige sind wirklich schlimm—wurden die Druckplatten nie korrigiert. Sie gingen nach dem Tode von Walsh (1766) an Hermond Wright, der sie um 1785, bis auf das Impressum unverändert, nachdruckte. Noch etwa 25 Jahre später waren sie in Gebrauch, wie die Ausgabe bezeugt 'Printed & Sold by [Thomas] Preston, at his Wholesale Warehouses, 97, Strand' (um 1810). In der Zwischenzeit waren zwei weitere englische Ausgaben erschienen, eine bei James Harrison als Teil eines *New Musical Magazine* [1784], die andere bei Samuel Arnold in Faszikel 131 seiner vollständigen Händel–Ausgabe (um 1793); beide basieren ziemlich eindeutig auf Walsh, jede ihrerseits mit weiteren Druckfehlern.

Drei andere Ausgaben des späten 18. Jahrhunderts sollten auch genannt werden, obwohl merkwürdigerweise nur die erste bei William C. Smith in seinem umfassenden Werk aufgeführt ist (*Handel: A Descriptive Catalogue of the Early Editions*, 1960, revidierte 2. Auflage 1970). Dabei handelt es sich um eine Sammlung von *Quatorze Fugues Pour Clavecin ou Piano* bei Imbault in Paris um 1790, die zusätzlich zu den hier zur Diskussion stehenden sechs Fugen noch fünf andere aus den *Suites de Pieces* enthält, dazu drei weitere für Tasteninstrumente bearbeitete aus op. 6 Nr. 1, Nr. 6 und Nr. 11. Die anderen beiden Ausgaben sind in Deutschland erschienen. Sie haben beide keine quellenkritische Bedeutung, können jedoch beträchtliches Interesse für sich in Anspruch nehmen, da beide textlich unabhängig sind nicht nur von den früheren Editionen bei Walsh (und Boivin/Le Clerc), sondern auch untereinander und bis zu einem gewissen Grade auch von den Handschriften-Quellen. Die erste (*VI Fugen / von / HENDEL / für / Componisten Organisten / und / Liebhaber der höhern Musik*) erschien 1787 in Darmstadt, vermutlich bei Krämer & Bossler, die zweite (*SIX FUGUES / pour le / CLAVECIN ou L'ORGUE / composées par G. F. Händel*) bei Leopold Kozeluch in Wien nur zwei Jahre später.[7] Von den verschiedenen Ausgaben des 19. Jahrhunderts kann nur der Text von Chrysander 1859 (in Band 2 der Ausgabe der Händel-Gesellschaft) wirklich Anspruch auf Wissenschaftlichkeit erheben, doch ging er, wie es heute scheint, von keiner der hier in Betracht gezogenen Originalquellen aus, sondern eher von der Peters–Ausgabe [1848] ('nouvelle revue et corrigé critiquement'), mit der sie faktisch identisch ist.

Editorische Methode

Mit Ausnahme des Malmesbury-Manuskripts, dessen abweichende Lesarten mir freundlicherweise von Terence Best mitgeteilt wurden, ist jede der oben genannten Quellen vom Herausgeber dieser Edition sorgfältig untersucht worden. Keine, nicht einmal das Autograph, ist in jeder Hinsicht genau. Den Vorrang behält daher die Ausgabe bei Walsh von 1735, die, wie bereits festgestellt, die Druckerlaubnis des Komponisten hatte. Dieser Text ist hier, von Fehlern bereinigt, wiedergegeben. Allerdings wurde eine erhebliche Anzahl von Pausen, Haltebögen, Vorzeichen und gelegentlich sogar Noten ergänzt aus denjenigen der anderen Quellen, die entweder früher oder so ziemlich gleichzeitig mit dem Druck sind und denen ein gewisses Maß an Autorität zugebilligt werden kann— am eindeutigsten natürlich das Autograph, aber auch (in absteigender Reihenfolge der Wichtigkeit) F2, F3, J und die Pariser Ausgabe von 1738. Diese Ergänzungen sind alle durch runde Klammern deutlich gekennzeichnet. Kleingedrucktes oder Angaben in eckigen Klammern sind Zusätze des Herausgebers; das gilt auch für alle durchstrichenen Haltebögen, Striche, die die Stimmführung anzeigen, und halbe eckige

[5] Ich bin Terence Best (Herausgeber der sechs Fugen in der Hallischen Händel–Ausgabe) sehr zu Dank verbunden, daß er mir die neuesten Informationen über die Schreiber und die Datierung der handschriftlichen Quellen zukommen ließ; soweit sie den Schreiber des Malmesbury MS betreffen, lösen sie die bisherigen Erkenntnisse in Bests eigenem Quellenverzeichnis (S. 177) ab.

[6] Vgl. Donald Burrows, 'Walsh's editions of Handel's Opera 1–5: the texts and their sources', in: *Music in Eighteenth-Century England*, hrsg. von Hogwood und Luckett (Cambridge, 1983), S. 87–90.

[7] Exemplare der Wiener Ausgabe befinden sich in der British Library (Signatur e. 438 b. [1]) und in der Sammlung von Gerald Coke, Esq., Bentley, Hants. Die Identifizierung von Kozeluch als Verleger verdanke ich Dr. Alan Tyson, All Souls College, Oxford. Von der Darmstädter Ausgabe (1787) gibt es in England kein Exemplar; dankenswerterweise stellte mir Herr Victor Cardell ein Xerox des Exemplars in der Yale University Music Library zur Verfügung.

trills are best taken short, starting in the usual Baroque fashion with the dissonant upper auxiliary.

Rather more troublesome are the suddenly interpolated Adagio markings at the end of all six fugues. In the manuscript sources, these appear only in nos. II and IV. It may be that the word 'Adagio' in this context is to be interpreted quite simply as the eighteenth-century equivalent of our 'molto allargando', but more likely perhaps that some gracing of the final bars is also implied. In each case, an editorial suggestion as to how this might be done is printed as an *ossia* to the passage in question, while nos. I and IV in particular need something rather more elaborate—a miniature cadenza in effect.

Except for Fuga V which, in the autograph, is headed 'Largo', none of the fugues has a tempo marking in any of the sources. As it happens, the John Reading copies of nos. II and III are both marked 'Vivace', but this, at this date, is not so much an indication of speed as of character.[8] Nevertheless, both movements are marked 'Allegro' in their orchestral versions, while no VI, in its trio sonata guise, carries the injunction 'Come alla breve'. But even this, some may think, is too fast for such a sustained and richly expressive piece. Also in some danger of being taken too quickly are nos. I and IV, both fugues to which Handel in an orchestral context might well have appended the marking 'A tempo ordinario'.

Considering the date of composition (1716–17), it is by no means inconceivable that the *Six Fugues or Voluntarys* were written with the 'noble chorus' of Father Smith's great organ in St Paul's Cathedral in mind. This instrument, the specification of which is given in Dr W. L. Sumner's classic study, *The Organ* (4/1973, pp. 407–8) was evidently a particular favourite with Handel who seems to have been a frequent visitor to the cathedral during this period.[9] There are, however, no registration marks in any of the sources. Similar movements in the published voluntaries of his English contemporaries are generally headed 'Full Organ' by which is meant some clear, bright-toned combination of stops (e.g. Great to 15th) which speaks promptly and sounds reasonably loud in context. While this will do quite nicely for nos. I and III, it does not suit the others equally well. Obviously the registration must vary with the character of the fugues, and this is especially important when the six are played as a set.

One other matter about which something ought perhaps to be said is the sheer technical difficulty which Handel's often very lively and sometimes widely spaced contrapuntal textures present. The problem of maintaining a reasonable legato in such circumstances was clearly recognized by eighteenth-century players also,[10] and those with small hands will find they occasionally need to 'cheat'. On a modern organ, this is easily done by using the pedals (coupled, but with no stops drawn).

H. Diack Johnstone
Oxford,
August 1985

[8] See Charles Cudworth, 'The Meaning of "Vivace" in Eighteenth Century England', in *Fontes Artis Musicae* xii (1965), pp. 194–5.

[9] See Sir John Hawkins, *A General History of the Science and Practice of Music* (1776), modern reprint of the 1853 edn. (New York, 1963), pp. 859 and 852 n.; also Charles Burney, *An Account of the Musical Performances . . . in Commemoration of Handel* (London, 1785), Sketch of the Life of Handel, p. 33 n. (a).

[10] See for example Nicolo Pasquali, *The Art of Fingering the Harpsichord* (Edinburgh, [1758]), pp. 21–5.

Klammern, die die Verteilung der Stimmen auf die Hände verdeutlichen. Vorzeichen in der Abschrift, die nach heutiger Gepflogenheit überflüssig sind (wobei Vorzeichen, die nicht ausdrücklich aufgehoben sind, durch den ganzen Takt Gültigkeit behalten), sind, ebenso wie einige überflüssige Pausen und Doppelhalsungen, stillschweigend weggelassen worden. Solche Vorzeichen, die in keiner der frühen Quellen enthalten sind, werden, demselben editorischen Prinzip gemäß, auch als Herausgeber-Zusatz gekennzeichnet. Alle anderen Abweichungen von der Walsh-Ausgabe sind zusammen mit einigen der wichtigeren Varianten in den Sekundärquellen im letzten Abschnitt mit der Überschrift 'Critical Commentary' verzeichnet.

Interpretation und Ausführung

In allen gedruckten und handschriftlichen Quellen ist das einzige benutzte Ornamentzeichen *tr* (oder ⁓) und das auch nur in Fuge I. Allerdings gibt es keinen Grund, warum nicht einige weitere Triller (und sogar der gelegentliche Mordent) ergänzt werden sollten, und so sind einige diesbezügliche Vorschläge in eckige Klammern gesetzt. Einige Spieler werden es vorziehen, sie nicht zu beachten, andere hätten wahrscheinlich gern noch mehr Hinweise dieser Art. Ausgenommen dort, wo Kadenztöne bereits in die Notation eingebaut sind (wei in Nr. I, T. 13 und T. 65), werden die meisten Triller am besten kurz gespielt und nach barocker Manier mit der dissonanten oberen Nebennote begonnen.

Problematischer sind die unvermittelt eingeschalteten Adagio-Bezeichnungen am Ende aller sechs Fugen. In den handschriftlichen Quellen kommen sie nur in Nr. II und Nr. IV vor. Möglicherweise ist das Wort 'Adagio' in diesem Zusammenhang schlicht als die Entsprechung des 18. Jahrhunderts zu unserem 'molto allargando' zu verstehen, vielleicht aber ist auch eine Verzierung der Schlußtakte gemeint. In jedem Fall ist eine Anregung des Herausgebers zur Ausführung als ossia-Version der entsprechenden Passage zugefügt, während besonders die Nrn. I und IV einen stärker ausgearbeiteten Schluß brauchen—praktisch eine Miniaturkadenz.

Mit Ausnahme der Fuge V, die im Autograph die Bezeichnung 'Largo' trägt, hat keine Fuge in keiner der Quellen eine Tempo-Angabe. Zwar sind John Readings Abschriften von Nr. II und Nr. III beide 'Vivace' benannt, doch ist dies zu dieser Zeit weniger eine Tempo-Angabe als eine Kennzeichnung des Charakters.[8] Dessen ungeachtet sind beide Sätze in ihrer Orchesterversion 'Allegro' überschrieben, während Nr. VI in ihrer Gestalt als Triosonate den Hinweis 'Come alla breve' trägt. Aber sogar dieses Tempo mag manchem zu rasch für einen so getragenen und ausdrucksstarken Satz vorkommen. In Gefahr zu schnell genommen zu werden, sind auch die Nrn. I und IV, beides Fugen, denen Händel in einem Orchesterzusammenhang die Bezeichnung 'A tempo ordinario' gegeben haben könnte.

Wenn man das Kompositionsdatum (1716/17) bedenkt, ist es keinesfalls unvorstellbar, daß die *Six Fugues or Voluntarys* geschrieben wurden im Hinblick auf den 'noble chorus' der großen Orgel von Bernard Smith in St. Paul's Cathedral. Dieses Instrument, das in Dr. W. L. Sumners ausgezeichneter Studie *The Organ* (⁴1973, S. 407–408) genau beschrieben ist, wurde offenbar von Händel besonders geschätzt; er scheint in dieser Zeit ein häufiger Besucher der Kathedrale gewesen zu sein.[9] Allerdings enthält keine der Quellen Registrieranweisungen. Ähnliche Sätze in den veröffentlichten Voluntaries seiner englischen Zeitgenossen sind allgemein mit 'Full Organ' überschrieben, womit eine helle, strahlende Registerkombination gemeint ist (z.B. Hauptwerk bis Superoktave 2'), die rasch anspricht und im Zusammenhang ziemlich laut klingt.

Während sie für Nr. I und Nr. III ausreichend sein mag, eignet sie sich nicht gleich gut für die anderen. Offensichtlich muß Registrierung dem Charakter der Fugen entsprechend unterschiedlich gewählt werden, was besonders wichtig ist bei einer Aufführung aller sechs Fugen als Zyklus.

Ein Wort sollte noch zu der erheblichen technischen Schwierigkeit gesagt werden, die Händels oft sehr lebendige und manchmal ausgedehnte kontrapunktische Satzgefüge bieten. Das Problem, unter diesen Umständen noch ein angemessenes legato beizubehalten, war auch von den Spielern des 18. Jahrhunderts klar erkannt worden,[10] und solche mit kleinen Händen werden gelegentlich 'mogeln' müssen. Auf einer modernen Orgel ist das durch Pedalgebrauch leicht zu bewerkstelligen (gekoppelt, aber ohne gezogene Register).

Übersetzung: Ruth Blume

H. Diack Johnstone
Oxford,
August 1985

[8] Vgl. Charles Cudworth, 'The Meaning of "Vivace" in Eighteenth Century England', in *Fontes Artis Musicae* 12 (1965), S. 194–95.

[9] Vgl. Sir John Hawkins, *A General History of the Science and Practice of Music* (1776), Reprint der Ausgabe von 1853 (New York, 1963), S. 859 and 852 Fußnote; ebenfalls Charles Burney, *An Account of the Musical Performances . . . in Commemoration of Handel* (London, 1785), Lebensabriß von Händel, S. 33 Fußnote (a).

[10] S. z.B. Nicolo Pasquali, *The Art of Fingering the Harpsichord* (Edinburgh, [1758]), S. 21–25.

SIX FUGUES OR VOLUNTARYS
for
Organ or Harpsichord

Edited by H. Diack Johnstone

GEORGE FRIDERIC HANDEL
(1685–1759)

FUGA I

Printed in Great Britain

OXFORD UNIVERSITY PRESS, MUSIC DEPARTMENT, WALTON STREET, OXFORD OX2 6DP

*On a modern organ, the l.h. of bb. 58–9 must be played an octave higher; alternatively the low *G*, may be played as *D* (as printed in the 1787 Darmstadt edition).

†*Adagio* would seem to imply a cadential flourish, perhaps as follows:

FUGA II

FUGA III

FUGA IV

Adagio

FUGA V

FUGA VI

CRITICAL COMMENTARY

The principal sources are here referred to as follows:

W Walsh edition (London, 1735)
P Boivin/Le Clerc edition (Paris, 1738)
A Autograph: British Library, MS RM 20 g. 14
F2 British Library, MS RM 18 b. 8
F3 British Library, MS RM 19 a. 3
J MS in the collection of the Earl of Malmesbury

Fuga I

bar 6, alto notes 1–2 tied in W (also in P)/12, r.h. note 1: downstem is editorial/17, last treble note: e'♮ in all sources; 1789 Vienna edn. however has e'♭, and this I believe to be correct (cf. Fuga V, b. 57). A originally had two quavers e'♮–d' at this point, but both the ♮ and the quaver d' were subsequently cancelled./19, last bass note: g in W (but f in P and all MS sources)/23, r.h. beats 1–2: ♪ in all sources save J/ 32, r.h. beat 4: e'♮ in all sources save F2; A not entirely clear, but the ♮ originally there appears to have been cancelled./42, alto note 3: downstem is editorial/48, treble note 5: a crotchet in all sources; 1787 Darmstadt edn. has ♪ ♪/59, bracketed alto note is in all MS sources/69, treble note 1: a minim in all sources (save Darmstadt)/ 70, l.h.: F2 adds d to final chord, F3 g.

Fuga II

In A, all ♮s save those in bb. 33 (l.h.) and 94 (l.h., note 3)—the latter omitted here as it is redundant—are written as ♭s, evidence perhaps that this fugue was composed somewhat earlier than some of the others (but see also nos. IV and V)./8, in W (and also P), treble note 1 is c'♯ and the first bass note a quaver rest (quaver a in A); the reading given here is that of F2, F3 (and 1789 Vienna edn.)/17, r.h. beats 1–2: ♪ in W, P, F3 and J; only A and F2 are correct/21, bass note 3: downstem is editorial/58, bracketed alto note is in all MS sources/67, treble note 1: ♪ (no rest) in W and P; F2 has ♪ ♪, F3 ♪ ♪, J ♩ ♩ and A o, while 1787 Darmstadt edn. reads: ♪ /104, tenor notes 3–4 transferred from treble to bass stave, hence the editorial ♯/111, alto note 3: ♯ in W (and P) only/112, bass note 1: d' in W (but b in P and all other sources)/123, beat 3: A and F2 both have Adagio (almost indecipherable in A) at this point; F3 on the other hand has 'Adg:' sited over beat 1/124, final r.h. chord: b', g', d' in W and in P.

Fuga III

25, bass note 1: A has lower octave D also/34, r.h. notes 5–6: g''–g' (treble), e''–b' (alto) in W, but as printed here in P/35, treble note 4: b'' in A/44, beat 1: alto note f and tenor d' are a' and f' respectively in A (and also in the John Reading copy of this piece: Dulwich College MS 92 d.)/48, bass note 3 omitted in A/52, alto notes 4–5: single crotchet f' in A/53, treble note 2: upstem is editorial/55–6, alto: bracketed notes in A only.

Fuga IV

The barring of this movement is erratic in all sources, and barlines missing in W are here drawn across each stave separately (see bb. 31–40 and 185–6). In A only the first 12 bars are barred in 2/4, and the rest as if in common time (C); all ♮s (save the one in b. 90) are here written as ♭s (cf. Fuga II and V)./35, bracketed treble note is in all MS sources (and also in 1789 Vienna edn.)/41, bass note 1: downstem is editorial/53, bass note 2: upstem in A and F2 only/57, alto note 1: d' in W and P, but correct in all MS sources/59–61, r.h.: ♪ in W and P/76, bracketed treble note is in all MS sources/90, bracketed alto note in A and F2 only/91, bass note 3: W has lower octave a also (c' in P)/113, bracketed bass note in A and F2 only/126, bracketed treble note in A and F2 only/126–7: blatant consecutive octaves in outside parts are present in all sources (cf. bb. 97, 149–51 and Fuga V, b. 71)/148, bracketed alto note is in all MS sources/158, bracketed alto note (head, no stem) in A only; F2 and J both have a corresponding dot here, but there is no following f' in J/159, bracketed tenor note is in A and F2 only/183: A originally had an additional g' in r.h. chord and an e added to l.h. octave, but these appear to have been cancelled. The word Adagio (very faintly written in A) is abbreviated 'Adg°.' in W and in F3; in A, F2 and F3, however, it is sited one bar earlier (in 182)./185–6: r.h. stave blank with figured bass only in W; also A, F3 and J (which omits figuring). The r.h. parts printed here are those of F2; P on the other hand reads as follows: ♪ with an additional b in the l.h.

Fuga V

A has tempo mark 'Largo', and all ♮s save those in bb. 13 (r.h. note 2) and 44 (l.h.) are here written as ♭s (cf. Fuga II and IV)./7, bracketed treble note in all MS sources save F3/8, bass notes 4–5: e'–d' in W (but correct in P)/16, bracketed tenor note is in all MS sources/19, beat 2: A has additional e' (crotchet) in alto/23, treble note 2: downstem is editorial/32, treble notes 1–2: tied crotchets (both d'') in W (and also P); all MS sources, however, have the reading printed here/40, treble beat 2: two quavers d''–e'' in A; this reading also, curiously, in the Israel in Egypt version of this movement./47, alto notes 1–2 tied in W only/71: consecutive octaves between bass and alto in all sources.

Fuga VI

9, bracketed alto note is in all MS sources; likewise the bracketed notes in bars 10, 41 and 45/10, tenor note 3: ♪ (no bass d) in both W and P/11, tenor note 1: dotted crotchet (no quaver rest) in A/14, last two bass notes: quaver b in A/23, last two treble notes: f'–g' in W, P and J (but correct in A and other MS sources)/ 31, bracketed alto note in all MS sources save F3/34, tenor note 5: a in W but c' in all MS sources/47, bracketed tenor note (present in all MS sources) is only a crotchet in F2 and J/52, treble beats 1–2: A reads ♪ but was originally ♪ /56, bracketed alto note is in P and all MS sources; in W, treble notes 5–6 have both up and downstems and there is no alto c'.